Adaptations

Emily Pinkerton

Nomadic Press
2018

This book was made possible by a loving community of family and friends, old and new.

Requests for permission to make copies of any part of the work should be sent to info@nomadicpress.org.

For author questions or to book a reading at your school, bookstore, or alternative establishment, please send an email to info@nomadicpress.org.

Published by Nomadic Press, 2926 Foothill Boulevard, Oakland, California, 94601
www.nomadicpress.org

First Edition
First Printing

Printed in the United States

Library of Congress Cataloging-in-Publication Data

Pinkerton, Emily 1985 –
Adaptations/written by Emily Pinkerton; illustrated by Arthur Johnstone
p. cm.
Summary: *Adaptations* is an exercise in envisioning the worst-case scenario and asking, "What next?" It explores concepts of alienation and survival in a world that's largely inhospitable, and what it means to be human once traditional mechanisms of control and safety cease to exist.

[1. POETRY / Subjects & Themes / Environment. 2. POETRY / Subjects & Themes / Politics. 3. POETRY / American / General.] I. Title.

2018958528

ISBN: 978-1-7323340-4-5

The illustrations in this book were created using gouache and ink on Canson paper.
The type was set in Garamond Premier Pro.
Printed and bound in the United States
Typesetting and book design by J. K. Fowler
Edited by Natasha Dennerstein and J. K. Fowler

for my father

CONTENTS

MAGNOLIA CITY SUMMER

Chemicals laced into our sunsets, burned our retinas
first, then our skin. Noxious orange, neon and toxic—
brilliant to watch in the humid evening air.
Houston, retch city, nice to meet you. Smell of rot
coming from what is brand new, petrochemical particulate
settling slowly over our modern homes. It's fucked up
but nobody's got a chip on their shoulder about it.
Too much rot for that. Too much chemical rain.
The fumes we breathed in and out burned us pure.
Newly mutated, we rise like steam, then disperse.
Refinery towers puff endless, orange-lit by flares—
always something to purify. I've got warped teeth
and no patience for weak souls, but I won't be cruel.
Made by polluted runoff, your byproduct—
this is an adaptation, you'll see.

OLIVIA ON A THURSDAY EVENING

A girl sitting on my stoop just arrived here
from the small town where I spent my childhood.
A place named after carbon and coal
we dug out of the muddy banks of the creek
in Miner park as a summer pastime.
She has the sweet moon-face
and eager voice of someone still naïve
in the face of hardship. I haven't lived
in that town for twenty years, haven't
talked to anyone I left behind and still
its dust carries down to find me. Here.
Here. Now, now.

WEATHERED MAN RECALLS THEIR FACES

I.

Round and smooth
Gently unlined terrain
Shaded lakeside in summer

II.

Ridged and hollowed
with the bright sheen of snow.
Mountainside in spring, evergreen
and spruce. Vital, constant, auroral.

III.

Pocked and cratered
from dynamite blasts.
The tunnel's open but
unreliable. You're on
your own there.

IV.

Cracked leather in a sandstorm.
Sure, dust catches in the folds—
It'll polish your teeth, too.

MARIPOSA GROVE

These are not the oldest living things.

    Visitors notice the roots   stay sparse, tolerant.

Quickly spread   impossible seedlings.

Snow blankets Mariposa Grove,

                these unnatural conditions.

DEAD RECKONING

Drive. When we get past the tree line
no map can help. I sense places in relation
to where I am. I can tell you where
you'll find what you're looking for:
the directions are in me, like instinct,
like bones.

WEATHERED MAN SPEAKS ON CLOSENESS

If you don't have a gun,
steel rebar and a strong arm
will do the job.

BIRDS

I. (Pigeon)

The pigeon huddled in the driveway
head buried in its chest
matted feathers puffed out
and I knew immediately it was dying.

I took two steps forward, stooped down
as if to ask: how are you feeling? are you ok?
As if I might pick it up and hold it in my hands
to feel it shiver, to see if it was still alive
if I could help.

I reached down, saw its dried shit beneath its feet
and knew. I didn't want to touch something
the life had already gone out of
so I walked away.

II. (Magpie)

I'm a different kind of bird.
A lost magpie that smashes into the window repeatedly
senseless and frenzied in flight, blood and bits of feather
left in cobweb cracks in the glass. I fly forward. I fly forward
toward the horizon, evermore frightened
and absolutely certain that the way out is through,
fixed on a horizon I cannot reach.
As for the open window I flew in through:
I'll fly through this glass before I go back that way.

FLIGHT PATTERNS

I.

I've been thinking
of flight this week
how it's shaped me.

what I leave out:
I touched moon soil
I cried for the shuttle

eyesore refineries
where father worked
and the fume smell

Columbia, luminescent
in multiple ion trails
moving eastward still.

II.

For a brief time
I flew.   joyful,
monumental—
after a while, I didn't.

in between chemtrails   I couldn't.
inventing reasons to be anywhere   I never wanted to;
but where   was   I was afraid of,
the Atlantic   up and down the coast.

no desire to ascend
on mapped patterns
a farewell: take flight—
came unglued.

III.

vapor trail overhead

I walked. gas and steam

writing chalk

blank blue slate.

leaves fall fluttering spinning

vortexes, orange and brown. breeze remnants

scatter

upward. They lingered

floated down

like confetti

everyone is already running.

stay.

UMTANUM RIDGE

I was good in bad conditions
and conditions were always bad.

We didn't know what to pray for then.
Rain to quell the heat. Peace to end the stench

Of sun-bloat and body-rot. More brains or more nerve.
Each new step was brittle and we chafed in the sun.

Conditions being what they were, we carried on—
Tumbleweeds scattering spores. Dust on the ridge.

AN INTERLUDE

Not feeling well. Been having nightmares
about an earth littered with thousands
of tiny syringes. I walked over them
barefoot. Does it mean I'm infected?
I should get tested. I wonder if the dead
ever smile. I can't stop thinking about it.

AN INVOCATION

                        Bluer than usual
it smelled like burnt synthetic fiber outside
it smelled like rotting kelp, sun-bleached, bacterial.
Waves built and broke quickly, oversaturated
brightening under whitecaps and foam
closed out   bluer than usual. Unwilling to risk
a new infection, I stayed onshore   wind-whipped, longing.
The blue-green jewel shining

SENSE OF DIRECTION

The map is only an outline. Trails cross-hatched
in thin lines, nothing more. No ornament or illustration
for rockslides blocking our path, cougars stalking the wooded route.
This, our hard journey toward a shadowed sense:
dim inkling, unshakeable dream. We move forward—
whether we die in the desert or the woods, doubled back
and hopelessly lost, we move forward. Hardwired pursuit,
like the taste for blood after a mean winter. Matted fur
& bared incisors move us on, the ink-drawn route not to scale.
Not the point. We were born, we stumble and soldier on—
good animals with good instincts, with no need for maps.

WEATHERED MAN SPEAKS ON WHAT IS ROTTEN

Strong stomachs
come from hunger—

Indiscriminate need
beyond taste or smell.

COYOTES

On the farm where my niece lives
coyotes are eating the sheep.

I always wanted to be a good sheep,
grazing calmly in the field.

Fuck it. The sheep are dead.
I can't pretend anymore. I want to live without hiding

Trickster eyes, bloody incisors. No more passing
As pet, always disappointing. No, I'm anything but.

I'm sorry for what flesh I tore. Predatory instincts.
I was never tame, I know.

VIABLE SEEDS

Forest floor: the heat
From a fire lighting
Leaf-litter. This dependency
On fires, deceptive. Here
The fallen. Weakened
By the massive hole
Viable seeds endure.

BAYOU AUTUMN

A poet asked, *Does Texas taste like heaven*
when it rains? The answer is *no*. It tastes
Like sludge and granite. Like bayou scum
and the sweet-smelling residue of plastic
polymers. The same stench they use
in port-a-john air fresheners, whenever the wind blows.
But sometimes it looks like heaven
the kind the Devil would create
to fool unsuspecting men. Spanish moss
in the cypress trees and the glassy water reflecting
big wide sky, gold-tinged, for miles
warm and inviting. While the egrets pace
in the reeds, alligators wait alongside.

AN AFTERWARDS

Autumn sunlight warms the garden and
I taste the first drops of blood in my mouth,
metallic like cold summer water
straight from the hose, its faint dirt smell
in the aftertaste.

ACKNOWLEDGEMENTS

Thanks

To my father, who gave me the grit and nerve to write these poems. To everyone who knew me in Texas, especially those who rode through the badlands with me. To Laura Wolfe, Sonya Vatomsky, Fisayo Adeyeye, and Barbara Tomash for reading early drafts and championing my work. To J. K. for giving it a home, and Natasha for excellent edits. To Vernon, Philip, MK, Fisayo, and Arisa for writing incredible works that inspire me. To the entire Nomadic family for welcoming me to share space with you.

Most of all, to you, the reader. You breathe magic into these words.

"Viable Seeds" and "Mariposa Grove" use a Yellowstone National Park brochure as their source text. The words contained within each poem were originally authored by park ranger Jon Kinney. Each poem recombines and lightly edits select words and phrases found in the brochure.

"Flight Patterns (I)" combines the author's original text with descriptions of the Columbia Shuttle disaster, including the phrase "multiple ion trails" from the associated Wikipedia entry (https://en.wikipedia.org/wiki/Space_Shuttle_Columbia_disaster).

Transfer, vol. 115 (2015): "Magnolia City Summer"
Noble/Gas Qtrly, issue 202.4: Electric Resistance (2015): "Flight Patterns (I-II)"
sPARKLE & bLINK, vol. 71 (2016): "Birds" and "Olivia on a Thursday evening"
Pith, issue 4 (2016): "Flight Patterns (III)"
BlazeVOX, vol.16, issue 1 (2016): "An Invocation" and an earlier version of "Mariposa Grove"
Noble/Gas Qtrly, issue 203.4 (2016): "Coyotes"
Foglifter, vol. 2, issue 1 (2017): "An Afterwards"

Raised in the shadow of Houston refineries, **EMILY PINKERTON** currently lives and writes in the San Francisco Bay Area. She holds an MA and MFA from San Francisco State University, and her writing has previously appeared in *ZYZZYVA, Juked, BlazeVOX, Pith, Hobart*, and *LEVELER*, among others.

She is the author of two previous chapbooks, *Natural Disasters* (Hermeneutic Chaos Press, 2016), and *Bloom* (Alley Cat Books, 2018).

More of Emily's publications can be found at thisisemilypinkerton.tumblr.com, and she tweets as @neongolden. Her favorite color is fog.